# Shirley
# Temple Black

# Shirley
# Temple Black

## Actor and Diplomat

### JEAN F. BLASHFIELD

Ferguson
*An imprint of* ☑®Facts On File

**Ferguson Career Biographies: Shirley Temple Black**

Ferguson
An imprint of Facts On File, Inc.
132 West 31st Street
New York NY 10001

**Library of Congress Cataloging-in-Publication Data**

Blashfield, Jean F.
 Shirley Temple Black: actor and diplomat/ by Jean F. Blashfield.
  p. cm. —(Ferguson's career biographies)
 Includes bibliographical references and index.
 ISBN 0-89434-338-6
  1. Temple, Shirley, 1928– —Juvenile literature. 2. Motion picture actors and actresses—United States—Biography— Juvenile literature. 3. Diplomats—United States—Biography— Juvenile literature. [1. Temple, Shirley, 1928– 2. Actors and actresses. 3. Diplomats. 4. Women—Biography.] I. Title.  II. Series.

PN2287.T33 B59 2000
  791.43'028'092--dc21
  [B]                                                                    00-037189

An Editorial Directions, Inc. Book.

Photographs ©: AP/Wideworld: 21, 23, 28–29, 39, 54, 62, 84, 87, 94, 97; Archive: 12, 15, 17, 72–73; Corbis: 8, 19, 26, 45, 48–49, 68–69, 76, 78, 91; Liaison: 34, 42–43, 60, 98.

Printed in the United States of America

RRD  10 9 8 7 6 5 4 3 2

This book is printed on acid-free paper.

# CONTENTS

# "SPARKLE, SHIRLEY"

As THE CAMERAS were about to roll on the movie set, Shirley Temple's mother would whisper to the child actress, "Sparkle, Shirley." The tiny girl knew then to lick her lips so they shone, put a smile on her face, and concentrate on remembering her lines and dance steps. Her sparkle paid off.

In the 1930s, curly-haired, talented, and adorable Shirley Temple was the biggest film star in the world, and perhaps the most envied and beloved little girl of all time. As an adult, Shirley Temple Black used what

*As a little girl, Shirley Temple followed her mother's advice. She knew how to sparkle.*

she had learned as a child, as well as her natural intelligence, to represent the United States in other countries as a diplomat.

## A Star Is Born

Shirley Jane Temple was born in Santa Monica, California, on April 23, 1928. She was the third child of Gertrude and George Temple. George was a bank teller who kept his job even when the Great Depression was at its worst. The depression followed a stock market crash in 1929. The world's economy was so bad that many people were out of work and starving.

Shirley had two older brothers, John (called Jack) and George Jr., (called Sonny). There were nine years between Shirley and her brother Sonny. Eventually, Sonny's health problems would determine much of what Shirley did as a grown-up.

With the older children busy with their own affairs, Shirley's mother had plenty of time to devote to her long-awaited daughter. Much of their earliest play involved music and movement. Her mother listened to her record player as she did her household chores. And as soon as Shirley could walk—which she did on tiptoes—she would follow her mother around, making up rhythmic steps to the music. She was dancing.

When Shirley was three and a half, her parents decided they had to find the money to send her to dancing class. Lessons at Meglin Dance Studios began on September 13, 1931. Shirley paid close attention in class and did all she could to perform the steps correctly. It was always important for her to please the adults in her life.

Shirley's dance classes were close to the Hollywood movie studios. Sometimes movie scouts visited looking for young talent. On the day her class was to receive such a visitor, neither Shirley nor her mother knew about the visit. All other children arrived dressed in their best clothes, but Shirley came in her usual blue overalls. She walked over to the movie scout and said hello, then went home. They heard nothing from the visit. Shirley knew her mother was disappointed.

A week later, a scout from Educational Studios came to the dance studio. This time Shirley hid under the piano, not wanting to disappoint her mother again. The scout saw her and called her over. Soon her phenomenal career began.

## One-Reelers

Educational Studios put tiny Shirley in a series of very short films called Baby Burlesks. They were known as one-reelers because they filled only one reel of film. Baby Burlesks were parodies of popular films with children playing adult parts. Shirley's first successful one-reeler, called *War Babies,* featured Shirley as a "vamp," wearing an off-the-shoulder blouse and a diaper with a huge pin in it. Her first words on screen were in French: *"Mais oui, mon cher,"* which means "Of course, my dear."

There were other short Baby Burlesks about Tarzan, politics, showgirls, and cowboys and Indians, all with Shirley wearing an adult costumes on top and a diaper.

Educational Studios offered Shirley her first contract. The law required agreements between studios and child actors to be approved by a judge so that the studios didn't take advantage of children. They had to guarantee three hours of real schooling and a limited numbers of hours of filming each day. Shirley received ten dollars a day for these early short films. Each film took about four days to make. There was no pay for rehearsing.

*Shirley in one of her many Baby Burlesks. These short films were spoofs of full-length movies.*

Gertrude nagged Jack Hays, the producer, to find Shirley more substantial roles that didn't require her to wear a diaper all the time. He found several small roles for her, including one in her first full-length film, *The Red-Haired Alibi.* Educational Studios then put Shirley in another series called *Frolics of Youth.* These films were all about one family and resembled a modern TV sitcom. Gertrude had hoped to get her daughter a role in the famed *Our Gang* comedies, but she didn't succeed.

Hays loaned Shirley to Paramount Studios for a Zane Grey story, *To the Last Man.* In this western, Shirley was listed in the credits of Shirley Jane Temple, the only time her whole name was used. While Shirley was working at Paramount, Winfield Sheehan decided to tell the press that Shirley was a year younger than she was, to make her seem even more special. The child was small for her age, so they could get away with the deception. Even Shirley didn't know her real age until she was a teenager!

Shirley was released from her contract in 1933 after playing several other small roles. With no major film possibilities in sight, it seemed Shirley's short-lived movie career was over. George Temple urged his wife to give up.

## The Big Break

One evening George and Gertrude took Shirley to see herself in *Frolics of Youth*. After the film, Shirley and her mother waited out front for her father to get the car. Shirley was humming to herself and absently dancing a few steps. A movie songwriter saw her and thought she was adorable. He asked her mother to bring the child to his office the next day. Gertrude was skeptical, but decided to take a chance.

Winfield Sheehan, head of production at Fox Pictures (which later became Twentieth Century-Fox), saw Shirley in the songwriter's office and enthusiastically signed her up. Shirley had her first lead in a feature film and a seven-year contract.

*Stand Up and Cheer* starred Warner Baxter and James Dunn. Shirley sang and danced in "Baby, Take a Bow," a big number near the end of the film. The movie audiences loved her. Word spread of the sweet, talented little girl and brought record crowds to theaters all over the country.

Paramount Pictures had the movie rights to a

*James Dunn with Shirley in* Stand Up and Cheer, *her first feature film*

story by Damon Runyan called *Little Miss Marker*. They had been trying to find just the right child to play in the story of a girl who is put up as security (a marker) for a loan at a racetrack. Paramount saw Shirley in *Stand Up and Cheer* and knew their hunt was over. They borrowed Shirley from Fox for the sum of $1,000 a week. Shirley was paid only $150 of that.

*Little Miss Marker*, released in 1934, was an immense success. This was followed immediately by Shirley's hugely successful performance in *Bright Eyes*. By then Shirley was earning $1,250 a week, with built-in increases to come. She was committed to making three pictures a year, as well as additional ones for Paramount. Fox, which had been on the verge of bankruptcy only two years before, was now flourishing—all thanks to Shirley Temple.

## Fame

Shirley took the movie world by storm. On February 27, 1935, she was given a small, special Oscar by the American Academy of Motion Picture Arts and Sciences. She was told that she was receiving it

*In 1935, Shirley received a small, special Oscar. Irwin Cobb presented it to her at the Academy Awards.*

because she had given "more happiness to millions of children and millions of grown-ups than any child of her years in the history of the world." But all she wanted was to leave the boring dinner and go home. (And later, she realized that she hadn't received a real Oscar. The Academy wouldn't remedy that until 1985.)

Winfield Sheehan recognized what a treasure the studio had in Shirley. He protected her and guided her career, though he would soon be replaced by Darryl F. Zanuck. A small bungalow was built for her on the studio lot. Everything in the little house was scaled to Shirley's size. There, Shirley and her mother could pretend that they lived a normal life in a house during the day, though she went to her real home at night.

That year, she was receiving letters from more than 5,000 fans each week. A special room in her own real house and a secretary were devoted to answering all the mail. Many fans requested photos of her, and Shirley had to spend long minutes every day posing for new ones. Other, older stars also wanted to pose with Shirley, because it was great publicity just to be seen with her.

Movie followed movie—eight released in 1934,

*Time with family. Shirley and her parents sometimes tried to get away for vacations together.*

three in 1935, four in 1936, two in 1937, two in 1938, and four in 1939. These were the years of the Great Depression, but people would still scrape together a few cents for a movie ticket, especially one starring Shirley Temple. It was impossible to worry or be sad when her smiling face appeared on the screen. People all over the world came to know her and love her. Every parent wanted their daughter to be just like Shirley, and their daughters wanted to be just like her, too.

One fan magazine said of Shirley, "It is no exaggeration to say that Shirley's charm has done as much to lift the world out of its depression, by lightening the hearts of all who see her, as any of the wordy conferences that have been held by statesmen all over the world."

Sometimes the fame could be overwhelming for Shirley. All her birthday parties were staged for publicity value, without any real friends. Her seventh birthday brought 135,000 gifts and cards. She received more than a 1,000 cakes from fans for her eighth birthday party. Shirley gave most of these birthday gifts to hospitals, children's homes, and other charities.

*Actress Grace Fields was one of the many celebrities who gathered for Shirley's eighth-birthday celebration.*

## Her Mother's Role

Gertrude Temple has sometimes been called a pushy stage mother, someone who forces a child into performing. But Gertrude worked very hard for Shirley and the entire Temple family. She was the one who coached Shirley on all her many lines. Gertrude saw that Shirley slept and ate well, learned her dances and songs, fixed her hair. It was Gertrude who made sure that the Temples remained a close-knit family.

Shirley's mother stayed on the set, relaying instructions from the directors because she was the only person Shirley would listen to. Gertrude read to her quietly during breaks and made sure she ate properly and was always dressed right. Gertrude Temple made most of Shirley's costumes in the early movies.

Gertrude also pinned curls into her daughter's hair before each filming session. Shirley told *People* magazine that as a child she had to have her hair set in pincurls every night—"exactly 56, so it would match the scenes we'd shot the day before." Children everywhere yearned for such curls, and many mothers tried their best to duplicate them on their own daughters.

*With Mom on the set. Shirley often recited her lines for her mother before she faced the cameras.*

## Singing and Dancing

Shirley Temple was very bright and naturally talented. She amazed people by having perfect pitch when singing, even as a very young child. She learned roles, songs, and dances quickly. Shirley also had a long memory and could repeat them for months afterward.

During her earliest years, of course, Shirley could not read. Her mother always read the script to her at night, playing all the parts except Shirley's. The child gradually learned everyone's part, so that when she was on the set, she would often prompt other actors with their next lines. Some of these older actors appreciated her help. Others were offended.

People across the country learned the songs they had seen Shirley sing on the screen. Sometimes adult singers recorded the same songs to take advantage of their popularity. Her most famous song was "On the Good Ship Lollipop," by Richard Whiting. She sang it while dancing up and down the aisle of an airplane in *Bright Eyes.* Even today, more than sixty-five years later, people instantly recognize that song.

In the 1934 movie *The Little Colonel,* Shirley

danced with African-American vaudeville dancer Bill "Bojangles" Robinson for the first time. It was reported later that she learned his soft-shoe and tap numbers by closing her eyes and listening to his feet. She learned even the most complicated dances quickly. Directors rarely had to shoot a dance more than two or three times to get it right, which was very unusual in Hollywood.

Her most famous dance with Bojangles was in *The Little Colonel*. Shirley's character and the black servant in the old southern mansion danced up and down a flight of stairs together. She always got the rhythm and timing just right.

Shirley and Bojangles danced together in three more films and remained friends for a long time. She called him "Uncle Billy" and he called her "darlin'." He later opened a dance studio and declared himself "adopted grandfather" of Shirley's first child.

Some people at the time were shocked by the idea of a little white girl dancing with a black man. Shirley Temple Black would later say that she first learned about the hardships of racism towards African-Americans from knowing, loving, and watching the talented black dancer.

*Shirley and Bojangles made three films together, and they became good friends.*

## Shirley's Day

California law required child actors to be given lessons three hours each day. Starting in 1935, Shirley was taught by Frances Klampt. "Klammy" worked with her for years, making the necessary classes fun. She introduced Shirley to an imaginary classmate named Mergotroid.

Many years later, a child asked Shirley how she learned so much about the world. She replied, "Every time a foreign visitor would come to my studio to visit me, [Klammy] would give me a one-week assignment about the visitor. This generated my great interest in the world and the people."

For a movie called *Stowaway*, Bessie Nyi, a student at UCLA taught Shirley some Chinese phrases. Years later, when she was a diplomat, she would remember some of the Chinese phrases.

There were often other children on the movie set, but they were usually so in awe of the famous little girl that they wouldn't play with her. Her stand-in was a little girl named Mary Lou Islieb. For fifteen years, Mary Lou would sit or stand in the places where Shirley would have to stand later, so the movie crew could get the lighting and camera angles right. Mary Lou and Shirley were friends, but they

*Stand-in Mary Lou Islieb (second from right) and her mother having lunch with Shirley (far right) and Mrs. Temple*

didn't get together very often. When Shirley was working, Mary Lou was off the set, and when it was time for Shirley to relax, it was usually when Mary Lou was working.

Shirley was still a little girl, and she wasn't always well behaved on the set. She tended to get involved in games of her own between filming takes. Sometimes she would wander out of earshot and wouldn't answer when called. Production assistants had to go looking for her. Also, the directors sometimes punished her and other children by giving them "time out" in an icy black box that must have been frightening.

## The Private Life of a Star

Shirley had a natural style on the screen. She had none of the overly cute little mannerisms and voice that child actors sometimes use. Fox was afraid that she might pick up some of these habits if she got too much praise or if she saw other children on film. Her contract called for her not to be praised except by her parents and the management. Unfortunately, this also meant that she had to eat lunch alone, instead of in the studio commissary with other actors. Actors, like people everywhere, wanted to compliment the charming child. Sheehan also wanted her diet closely supervised because she tended to get chubby.

Shirley was the studio's treasure. Anything that could be done to make sure that she was able to make more films was done. She even had her own doctor who planned her menus and exercise. This doctor believed especially in the value of spinach, so Shirley got more than her fair share of the nutritious vegetable.

Unlike most children, Shirley couldn't have missing teeth. If one fell out during filming, a fake tooth had to be fashioned for her to fill in the gap.

In 1999, Shirley described her childhood days: "When I got home from the studio after a day's work, I would put on my blue jeans and t-shirt and play with the neighborhood kids. I was a tomboy and a tree climber. I wondered why the other children didn't work. I thought everybody did. I had a private tutor for school and had three hours of school a day. I worked four hours in front of the camera and had one hour for lunch. It seemed easy at the time."

As she grew, she became aware that not all children worked so hard and had so little time to just play. Even though she was surrounded by people, she was often lonely.

In her autobiography, *Child Star*, Shirley Temple Black describes a car journey across the country with her parents during the summer of 1938. They were going to Canada to meet the world-famous Dionne quintuplets, the first set of five children to survive infancy. But every stop along the way had to be milked for its publicity value.

Shirley rode alone in the back seat of her parents' car. Behind them came a second car in which rode her bodyguard, Johnny Griffin (called Griff); Mabel, the Temple's maid; studio publicists; baggage; and a large supply of Shirley Temple photographs and souvenirs to give away.

Writers have often implied that little Shirley was mistreated by being "forced" to work so hard. Other stars have spoken bitterly about their famous childhoods. Shirley later acknowledged that "any star can be devoured by human adoration, sparkle by sparkle."

Loraine Burdick, author of *The Shirley Temple Scrapbook*, wrote, "To each person who was able to get to her after an appearance, the knowledge that they had seen her, heard her, or touched her was an unforgettable experience. But to Shirley Temple it was eternal hardship."

## Building on Shirley's Fame

Ideal Novelty and Toy Company (later called Ideal Toy Corporation), made several dolls of different sizes that looked like Shirley Temple. More than a million and a half Shirley Temple dolls were sold. Today, they are among the most collectible dolls ever made. This doll opened a floodgate of toys, games, clothing, and food products with Shirley's name on them. Usually, Shirley was photographed for advertisements for the products, so when she wasn't on a movie set or in class, she was trying on clothing and being photographed or was singing on the radio.

Many of her ads and special appearances were not for making money, but for good causes such as the March of Dimes and the National Safety Council. When Shirley spoke, people listened. Because of such childhood experiences, the adult Shirley was fully aware of the importance of doing volunteer work for charitable causes.

Shirley needed a time and place to be a child instead of an actor. Some people were outraged at

*Shirley Temple starred with Victor McLaglen in* Wee Willie Winkie, *an adaptation of a Rudyard Kipling story.*

the cost when she was given a large, expensive playhouse on the grounds of her parents' home, but she had to have a special place to play on her own. She had become so popular that she could not safely use the beach at Santa Monica near her parents' home.

## The End of the Heyday

Most of Shirley Temple's movies were centered around the antics and love of an adorable child who causes an ill-tempered adult to soften. Everything ends happily, with Shirley singing and dancing all the way. The permanently popular *Heidi* was a good example.

The studios even had whole teams of writers whose only job was to write new plots for Shirley. In one film, *Wee Willie Winkie,* they changed the plot of Rudyard Kipling's story so that the little hero was a heroine.

# THE IN-BETWEEN YEARS

B Y 1939, AUDIENCES began to tire of films with sentimental plots. Shirley was beginning to reach the age where she was no longer so adorable. She was turning into an adolescent, and audiences weren't ready to see the adored child star grow up.

Rather than have Shirley gradually disappear into bad pictures, her parents bought out her contract with Fox for $250,000. The Temples decided it was time their daughter had a private life when she entered junior high school. She was twelve years old, and for the first time in her life, Shirley Temple was going to a school with other children. She attended Westlake School for Girls, an exclusive private school.

For the first time since she began working as a toddler, Shirley wasn't under contract to a studio. But that situation didn't last long. Metro-Goldwyn-Mayer (MGM) signed her to a new contract at the end of 1940, one that she would fulfill by acting during school vacations.

Shirley got to do all the regular things with her school friends. She and a gang of about a dozen girls went to dances called sock hops and movies, wrote letters, and studied together.

In school, Shirley had trouble at first with math. She had always disliked it, and Klammy had not pushed her to learn it. She also was used to displaying her knowledge in conversation with her teacher. She found it hard to have to write what she knew rather than talking it through.

Although Shirley was no longer the blond curly-top that people remembered so fondly, she was growing up to be a striking young woman. She reached a height of 5 feet, 2 inches (157 centimeters). Her hair straightened and turned dark brown

*Shirley with Harold Bocquet, the director of* Kathleen. *The film was not received well by the public.*

with reddish highlights. She still had two distinct dimples in her cheeks. She always seemed to be smiling, even when she was relaxed. She didn't realize it until a teacher said it was "weird," and that she shouldn't smile all the time.

## Making Movies during School

MGM tried to get Shirley for the role of Dorothy in *The Wizard of Oz,* but Fox would not release her from her contract. MGM also had Judy Garland (who ultimatly played the role of Dorothy), as well as Mickey Rooney. There was a limit to the number of good scripts they could find to keep their three teenage stars busy.

Shirley made only one film for MGM, called *Kathleen.* Unfortunately, it was another story of an young girl trying to soften the heart of an ill-tempered adult. No one, not even the audience, was happy with the result.

Though MGM gave her no more movies, other studios were willing to take a chance with the adolescent Shirley Temple. She was never lacking in scripts.

The publicity department at United Artists claimed that she was first kissed by a young man her own age in *Miss Annie Rooney,* which perked up public interest again for a while. She later confessed in her autobiography that she had actually been kissed some weeks before on a blind date with a boy from a nearby boys school "on the lips, in a horse corral."

She considers *Kiss and Tell,* released in 1945, the best of her so-called grown-up pictures. However, Columbia Pictures had to have the studio's writing staff fix the script because it was regarded as too sexy for the child star. Shirley Temple's last movie was released in 1949. It was a sequel called *A Kiss for Corliss.*

During this time, Shirley still did a lot of volunteer work, especially during World War II (1939–1945). Her efforts took her all over the United States and Canada. She also made numerous visits to hospitals, cheering wounded soldiers, many of whom were great fans.

She was popular with many of the young men who had gone to fight in the war. While some men had pin-up pictures of Betty Grable and other sexy adult stars, others kept pictures of Shirley Temple. She reminded them of the girl next door or their kid sister.

*On the set of* A Kiss for Corliss, *a sequel to* Kiss *and* Tell. *The film also starred David Niven (left).*

## The Wrong Marriage

Somehow, through all the work and volunteering, Shirley managed to graduate from Westlake School in June 1945. She did it with an engagement ring on her finger.

She had met Sergeant John (called Jack) Agar when he was twenty-three years old and she was sixteen. He was a physical education instructor in the Army Air Corps. The son of an old family from Chicago, Illinois, and the brother of a classmate of Shirley's, he was 6 feet, 3 inches (191 cm) tall and very handsome.

While she was excitedly playing Jack against another longtime boyfriend, he startled her by saying that he might be sent overseas. He asked that she marry him before he went.

She accepted Jack's engagement ring but said they must wait several years before marrying. Shirley changed her mind when she realized that he might actually be sent away.

On September 19, 1945, Jack and Shirley were married in an ornate church wedding. Even the governor of California attended along with famous movie moguls.

Parents everywhere had held Shirley Temple

*On her wedding day. Shirley married Jack Agar when she was only seventeen years old.*

up to their own daughters as an example. Now they had to accept the fact that she was barely seventeen and getting married.

Even during Shirley and Jack's wedding, some of the people from the film company noted that Shirley's new husband was good-looking, with an appeal that the public would notice. They went after him to become an actor. He was delighted with the idea, though he had sworn to Shirley he wasn't interested.

After Jack was released from the service, he and Shirley made a movie together called *Fort Apache* starring John Wayne and Henry Fonda. They followed it up with *Adventure in Baltimore.*

Almost from the time of the wedding, Shirley had doubts about marrying Jack Agar. He had said he had no interest in Hollywood, yet he became an actor. He loved parties and the whole Hollywood scene. He especially liked to chase other women. On top of it all, he drank too much.

It was unlikely that the two could ever have had a happy marriage. They were followed everywhere by reporters and photographers, and Jack himself was delighted with being regarded as a Hollywood heartthrob.

Every stage of Shirley Temple's life from her very earliest years had been announced in the headlines of movie magazines and newspaper gossip columns around the country and around the world. Her first pregnancy also was announced with great glee. Jack and Shirley's daughter, Linda Susan, was born January 30, 1948.

Sadly, just eighteen months later, nationally syndicated gossip columnist Louella Parsons announced that Shirley Temple was divorcing husband Jack Agar. The marriage, Shirley said, "just should never have happened." Shirley and Jack's divorce became final in 1950.

Jack Agar was quite good as an actor, but he remained a much sought after popular leading man only until he became alcoholic. Eventually he overcame his alcoholism and made more than fifty movies, most of them low-budget horror and western films.

During the years of her marriage to Jack Agar, Shirley continued to act. In addition to the two films with her husband, she made six other films before their divorce. Shirley Temple retired as a movie actress at the young age of twenty-one and she never made another movie.

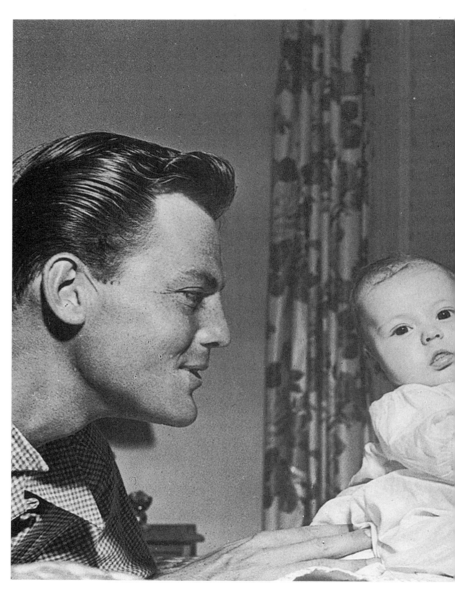

*Shirley with Jack and their daughter, Linda Susan. The baby was born in January 1948.*

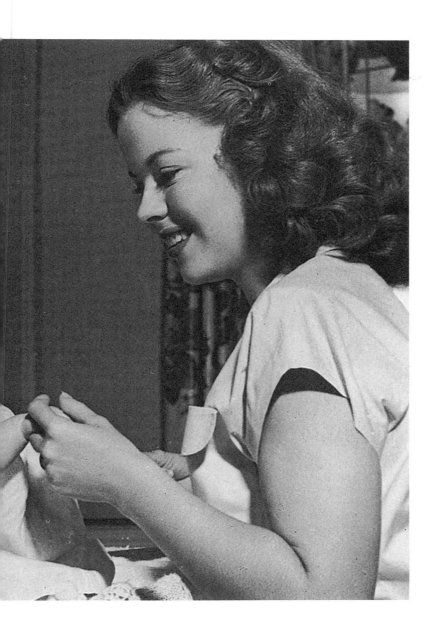

## Looking Back

Child stars have been popular with American audiences since long before the movies. Fans seem to get great satisfaction out of seeing photos of their favorite celebrities or reading about them and their private lives.

Shirley Temple was replaced in public adoration by several new child stars. Elizabeth Taylor, for example, was a huge hit in 1944's *National Velvet*. Margaret O'Brien became a star in the wartime tearjerker *A Journey for Margaret*. Shirley Temple wrote a magazine article of advice for Margaret based on her own experience.

Of course, child stars always grow up, and very few of them make the transition to adulthood smoothly. Some who have been unable to cope with being unknown as adults have committed suicide or committed crimes and ended up in jail.

Shirley Temple's family and her own ambitions made it possible for her to give up films without any terrible psychological problems. Her main ambition, despite her bad experience with Jack Agar, was still to marry, raise a family, and become an average person.

Shirley Temple, however, would never be average no matter how long or how hard she tried. As she left her career in films, Shirley would soon marry again and have that part of her life's dream come true.

# THE FAMILY
# YEARS

ONCE HER MOVIE career was over and the divorce final, Shirley, her parents, and daughter went on vacation to Hawaii in 1950. There, she met Charles Black, a young naval officer. Later, Shirley said that it was love at first sight, especially when she learned that he had never seen one of her movies.

Charlie was from an important family in San Francisco, California, and had degrees from both Stanford University and Harvard Business School. He served with the U.S. Navy during World War II and was in Hawaii

*Shirley with Charles Black, who would become her second husband. She loved that he had never seen any of her films.*

working with a pineapple company and enjoying the island's waves that make surfing there famous.

Before the end of the year, Shirley, married Charlie. This time, Shirley was married more quietly, in the home of Charles Black's parents in Monterey, California. Again, she gave up acting to take care of her new family.

## Financial Affairs

A few months after her marriage, Shirley was legally able to take control of her own money. Shirley had earned more than $3 million since starting in the movie business. She had never paid the least attention to her finances.

Ever since she started making money as a child, her father, George Temple, had acted as her financial manager. He and an acquaintance had set up a company to manage actors' business affairs, and Shirley was their first client.

Unfortunately, the ex-banker acquaintance wasn't as good as he thought. When Charlie and Shirley confronted her father, they learned that he had squandered most of her earnings in bad investments. He had not even followed the court order that required funds to be put into a trust for her. For almost twenty years of work, she had less than $60,000 left.

Earlier, Jackie Coogan, the first great child star of movies, had found that his mother and stepfather had squandered the millions that he had made in films. As an adult, he sued his mother to get what money was left, but the movie studios were so shocked that he would sue his own mother that he was banned from working.

Shirley later wrote, "For reasons some may find inexplicable, I felt neither disappointment nor anger. Perhaps years spent ignoring such matters had insulated me from disillusion." She decided that the money was gone and her relationship with her father was more important: "Picking over such corpses of the past is like the task of a carrion crow, disheartening and fruitless."

The Blacks agreed to forget the money. She was able to forgive her father and in later years, he and her mother came to live with them. The lost money was never mentioned.

## To Washington, D.C.

Charles Black was recalled to the U.S. Navy during the Korean War and stationed in Washington, D.C.

Since neither Shirley nor Charlie had much money, they lived in quiet, rather shabby circumstances in the capital until their California house sold and they were able to move out to the Maryland suburbs.

Shirley Temple did not go unnoticed in Washington. It made the newspapers when she got a parking ticket. She was often invited to embassy and Capitol Hill receptions that a lowly naval officer's wife would not ordinarily have attended.

These were the early days of television, and reporters often asked what she thought of seeing herself as a child on TV. As a mother, housewife, and charity volunteer, she had mentally separated "little Shirley" from Shirley Temple Black. She told the reporters, "She is a relative, and nobody knows her better than I. But what she does is her business, and what I do is mine. We are mutually supportive."

Since early childhood, Shirley was busy doing things for other people. She appeared at fund-raising events. She sent toys and gifts from fans to hospitals. Her volunteer attitude did not stop when she was an adult. Bess Truman, the wife of President Harry Truman, invited Shirley Temple Black to participate in some fund-raising that received so much personal publicity that Shirley's daughter, Susan, was threatened with kidnapping.

Shirley became more and more involved with Washington politics, especially in the presidential election of 1952, when General Dwight D. Eisenhower and Adlai Stevenson ran for president. She found the politic fascinating and often accepted invitations to Republican functions.

## Multiple Sclerosis

In 1952, just after Shirley's second child, Charles Jr., was born at the naval hospital in Maryland, Shirley's brother Sonny suffered a blood clot in the brain. It left him partially paralyzed. Sonny had symptoms that doctors determined were a nerve disease called multiple sclerosis, or MS.

Shirley joined the local MS Society to learn more and to help raise funds for fighting the fatal disease. Soon she became a national chairperson of volunteers of the National Multiple Sclerosis Society. Shirley discovered that she had a talent for fundraising. She traveled frequently to medical centers around the world to find out what was happening in MS research in other countries.

## Back to California and Acting

When Charles Black was released from the U.S. Navy in 1953, the family moved back to Los Angeles. There Charlie went to work for a television station. Shirley's third child, Lori, was born the following year. Soon the family got the opportunity to return to northern California, where they have lived ever since.

Charlie went to work for the Stanford Research Institute, and then moved into businesses related to oceanography. Most recently, he has worked on projects with Robert Ballard, the discoverer of the wreck of the *Titanic*.

Shirley cooked meals, decorated, helped at her kids' schools, entertained, and continued to carry out many volunteer activities, supporting the MS Society, the arts, and environmental causes. She also stayed up-to-date on national and international events. But this wasn't quite enough for someone who had been working regularly since she was three years old.

Among the things the family did together was watch old Shirley Temple movies on television. After a time, Shirley began to wonder if she should

*At home with her children Charles and Lori. Motherhood was always a priority for the former child star.*

return to acting, even though she was in the habit of refusing the many offers regularly made to her.

In 1957, she met a television producer at a dinner party. They had an animated discussion about fairy tales and their importance to children. A few weeks later, he called her with an idea for a television series in which Shirley would retell classic fairy tales and even occasionally act.

The show was called *Shirley Temple's Storybook*. Each of Shirley's children appeared in a Mother Goose program, though only Charles Jr. had a speaking role. The television program lasted a year and was very popular. After almost twenty years, Shirley Temple clothing and dolls were again being sold.

Live television was a completely new experience for the former film star. There was no chance to refilm scenes that didn't go right. One of the pleasures was being able to wear beautiful, one-of-a-kind gowns.

In the autumn of 1961, a new show, *Shirley Temple Theater*, began. It featured tales by a variety of authors. These were full-hour shows, broadcast when color TV was still quite new.

*On the set of* Shirley Temple's Storybook. *This episode starred Charlton Heston (left) and Claire Bloom (right).*

During this period, Shirley made guest appearances on television variety shows. She made even more frequent public appearances in person, as a speaker for the Republican Party. These appearances would change her life.

# INTO POLITICS

**O**NE OF THE first Shirley Temple one-reelers was a satirical comedy called *Polly Tix in Washington*. As an adult living in Washington, D.C. Shirley Temple Black had become interested in the reality of politics and international relations.

In 1952, Dwight D. Eisenhower was elected president. Back in California, she and her husband had supported other Republican politicians. In 1960, when President Eisenhower's two terms were ending, she was determined to do whatever she could to get another Republican, Richard Nixon, elected to the White House.

Shirley was very good at getting people to vote. She was responsible for San Mateo County in California voting Republican, even though Nixon lost the race nationally to Democrat John F. Kennedy. Shirley Temple, known previously as an actress, was becoming known as Shirley Temple Black, Republican vote-getter.

## Journey to the Soviet Union

Shirley Temple Black's main interest was still multiple sclerosis. In 1960, she met the Soviet premier, Nikita Khrushchev, at a reception in San Francisco. He was delighted to meet Shirley Temple. Even Russians knew who she was. Five years later, she decided to go to the Soviet Union to find out how multiple sclerosis was treated there. She hoped that the Soviet Union and the United States might share their research into the terrible disease.

This was her first trip to Europe, and she found that it was just as hard to stay out of the public eye in London and Moscow as it was in Washington. She tried to reach Khrushchev but failed. She did manage to locate a MS researcher she had heard about. As a result of this meeting, she helped to found the International Federation of Multiple Sclerosis Societies.

That same year, 1965, she gave some thought to returning to television. Because of its political theme, she willingly made a pilot, or test film, for a TV series called *Go Fight City Hall*. However, no sponsor was willing to pay for a program starring the adult Shirley Temple.

## Republican Black

After her trip to the Soviet Union, Shirley came to feel that democracy in the United States was very important. Mrs. Black began to make more public appearances on behalf of the Republican Party.

In 1966, Republican Ronald Reagan ran for governor of California. He too was a former actor and had to overcome public skepticism about his ability to govern. Reagan had appeared with Shirley in the 1947 film, *That Hagen Girl*. She made many appearances on his behalf and was credited with helping to get him elected. He appointed her to several statewide commissions.

She remembered that, as a child, she had met the famed pilot, Amelia Earhart, shortly before

Earhart mysteriously disappeared over the Pacific Ocean trying to fly around the world. The pilot had told her that "a woman could do anything she wanted to do with her life if she really worked hard."

Shirley decided that she would run for Congress

*Shirley Temple Black with her family as she admitted defeat in her 1967 campaign*

to represent San Mateo County in 1967. There were eleven other candidates. The election was tough because she began her campaign too late. Her campaign staff was inexperienced, and other candidates made fun of Shirley and her *Good Ship Lollipop*. Even

so, she came in second. Even though she came close to her goal, Shirley decided that she would stick to helping other people get elected.

In 1968, Richard Nixon ran for president again. She spoke for him throughout the country. Her name brought in audiences, but her political knowledge made them listen. Unfortunately for Shirley, many people only remembered her fondly as little Shirley Temple. They gave her so many affectionate squeezes that she always returned home bruised.

## Escape from Prague

No matter what else was going on, Shirley continued to make what efforts she could in the fight against multiple sclerosis. In 1968 she went to Czechoslovakia in Eastern Europe to organize that Communist nation's entry into the International Federation of Multiple Sclerosis Societies.

On the day before she was to leave Prague, the capital of Czechoslovakia, she was supposed to visit with First Secretary Alexander Dubcek. The meeting was canceled at the last moment because Dubcek had become involved in an "emergency," as the message she received put it.

Before dawn the next day, she woke to learn that

an army was invading the city. The Soviet Union had come to take over Czechoslovakia. Shirley was trapped in her hotel.

Some federation members came to help her get out of the country, but Shirley decided to go to the U.S. embassy. The next morning, a convoy of cars left the embassy for the border with West Germany, which was 71 miles (114 kilometers) away.

It took five hours for the cars to go the distance that should have been traveled in little more than an hour. Every few minutes they were stopped by Soviet troops. Shirley never knew when they might be shot at or bombed by one of the jets flying overhead. But the convoy made it safely to the border.

## To the United Nations

When Richard Nixon was elected president in late 1968, he thanked Shirley Temple Black for her efforts on his behalf by naming her one of five U.S. delegates to the United Nations General Assembly. Sometimes delegates who were also celebrities don't do any actual work, but Shirley was very interested in international relations, especially after her experience in Czechoslovakia.

*At the United Nations. Shirley Temple Black was appointed to the General Assembly by President Richard Nixon.*

Eleanor Roosevelt, the wife and widow of President Franklin D. Roosevelt, had been one of Shirley Temple Black's heroines, ever since they had met when she was a child. As an adult, she grew to admire Mrs. Roosevelt's work at the United Nations and her concern for human rights. She was honored to be following in Mrs. Roosevelt's footsteps at the UN.

Shirley and Charles took an apartment in New York City near the United Nations. At this time, he was working all over the world on oceanographic research projects, so it didn't much matter where they lived. The children were almost grown and could cope without constant attention.

Shirley Temple Black was appointed to the Social Humanitarian and Cultural Committee. She was involved in education, refugee problems worldwide, and the environment.

Later she told of how a child star came to be accepted as a serious UN delegate. "When I was a delegate at the United Nations I was given thirteen assignments for the 24th General Assembly. I learned later the average workload was four assignments. So they were really testing me. I took books back to my hotel in New York every night and studied late. When they saw that I did my homework and was a serious representative I was accepted."

She began to move beyond her reputation as Shirley Temple child actress to make a new reputation as a earnest negotiator. In a interview years later, she said, "The name has helped a great deal in opening doors—but, once the door is opened, I have to be able to do my job well. Otherwise, the door would close."

## The Environmental Conference

In 1970, Shirley Temple Black was given a new post, one that would involve her in the environmental problems of the world. The UN Conference on the Human Environment was to be held in Stockholm, Sweden, two years later. Shirley became the deputy to the chairman of the U.S. delegation. Because the conference itself would last only two weeks, all the delegations had to work hard to prepare for it. She spent weeks at a time in New York working with the delegation, on which she was the only woman.

The conference itself, held in 1972, turned very political, with many delegates from other countries criticizing the United States. On the last day, Delegate Black was asked to speak to the thousands of

*Delegate Black at an environmental conference in Stockholm. She gave serious attention to her work for the United Nations.*

people assembled—with less than two hours' notice. She spoke briefly, calling for "rational management of our common resources."

Despite the political fighting, the Stockholm meeting was an important milestone for increasing awareness of environmental problems. It led to the eventual creation of the United Nations Environment Program.

## A Terrible Interruption

While attending one of the environmental meetings, Shirley found a strange lump in one breast. Before having surgery to remove the lump, she went to the Soviet Union for two weeks of meetings. Somehow she managed to keep her mind on the conference and not the terrifying possibility that she might have cancer. The lump turned out to be cancer, and Mrs. Black had the breast removed. At that time, women did not talk about such operations because they were thought to be too terrifying and private.

Shirley bravely decided to let the public know, thinking that secrecy just made the operation worse. She called in the press, announced her operation, and allowed pictures to be taken of her in her hospital bed. She was the first public figure to announce

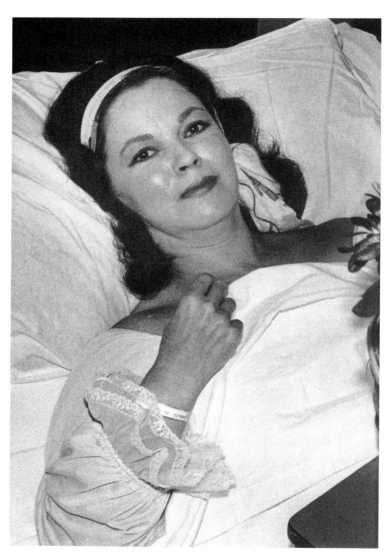

*Recovering after surgery. Shirley Temple Black kept no secrets about her breast cancer.*

that she had had a breast removed. Since then, many woman have gone public with the information. The surgery, as terrible as it is, is no longer regarded as something shameful and secret.

As Shirley was recuperating, Richard Nixon was reelected president. Like the rest of the United States, she did not know that some of the people who had worked for Nixon had broken the law and then had broken more laws to cover up what they had done. This came to be called the Watergate scandal, after a hotel in Washington where Nixon supporters committed burglarly. Eventually, President Nixon was forced to resign.

Except for some work on environmental quality in Washington, Shirley Temple Black remained a private person for the next two years. But the government's leaders had not forgotten her. She was about to take her political skills on the road to Ghana.

# MADAME AMBASSADOR

I N HER MAGAZINE article of advice to Margaret O'Brien, teenaged Shirley Temple had written, "Study and become as well informed as possible because as an actress you'll meet a great many outstanding people, including scientists, statesmen, writers and artists, and you'll want to speak and understand their language." Little did she dream that her childhood experiences would be useful when she began to represent the United States of America.

When Shirley Temple Black was named to top diplomatic posts, many people wondered whether "Curly Top" would actually have to do any real work. Perhaps, they thought, she would be just another celebrity who was all fame and no brains. It turned out that she had the skill, humor, intelligence, perception, and determination to make a great diplomat. Shirley was a diplomat longer than she was an actress. She served in various international posts under Presidents Richard Nixon, Gerald Ford, Ronald Reagan, and George Bush.

## To Ghana

Gerald Ford became president upon the resignation of Richard Nixon in August 1974. One of his first tasks was to name ambassadors. Most ambassadors come from the ranks of career diplomats in the U.S. Foreign Service, but every president has the right to appoint ambassadors from outside the Foreign Service. Some presidents make appointments to repay generous campaign contributors.

Many thought this was the case with Shirley Temple Black, but she had never contributed much money. Instead she had considerable experience of Africa from her years working with the United Nations. President Ford said that since Ghana is a matriarchal society, where women have considerable power, it seemed appropriate that a woman be named ambassador.

On September 20, 1974, Shirley Temple Black was sworn in at the U.S. State Department. She then attended many briefings on Ghana specifically and Africa in general. She also had to renew her knowledge of French and learn some words in several local Ghanaian languages.

It was a tough assignment. Ghana had a history of government takeovers since Kwame Nkrumah had freed it from British colonial rule in the 1950s. When Shirley arrived in Accra, the capital, the country was governed by a military dictator, Colonel I. K. Acheampong. He and his friends were stealing all the wealth of the country. Shirley herself was under a death threat by a terrorist group the whole time she was there, but she decided to ignore it.

Much of the job of the embassy was to grant U.S. visas to the many Ghanaians who wanted to flee their poverty-stricken country for the United States. A great deal of the ambassador's work was done during social occasions, which usually meant fourteen-hour days for the ambassador.

Her daughter Susan later wrote an article about her mother's life in Ghana. "Being an ambassador is

*Black was appointed ambassador to Ghana by President Gerald Ford. She accepted the post with enthusiasm.*

hard work, but Mom has risen to the challenges with an enthusastic and adventurous spirit, using a feminine approach uniquely her own. The diplomatic life is definitely Mom's element, even though her means of accomplishing the ends do not always follow tradition."

Among Shirley's non-traditional ways of dealing with the representatives from other countries was playing chess and holding film parties. In these ways, she established relations with China and the Soviet Union at at time when both countries were enemies of the United States.

In April 1976, she received two letters, one disappointing and one thrilling. The first was from the State Department, telling her that her time as ambassador was over and she was to return to the United States. The second was from President Ford, appointing her the first ever female U.S. Chief of Protocol for the White House.

## Chief of Protocol

Protocol is the traditions and rules for the conduct of important leaders visiting Washington, D.C., and for America's representatives abroad. Protocol considers the traditions of all the countries involved, who is superior to whom, in what order various visitors are to be shown in, what titles to be are used, and so on. Chief of Protocol is an important position for both national and international relations. As a little girl, Shirley had met many different kinds of people and knew how to make everyone feel at ease.

Working with a staff of more than three dozen people, she was in charge of teaching new ambassadors and their wives the customs that they would encounter in the countries to which they were to be sent. They had to know how to act so that they would not offend the people of other nations.

*At a hearing before being approved as chief of protocol. Shirley Temple Black was appointed to this position when her time as ambassador to Ghana was over.*

Shirley's daughter wrote about something she had to know in Ghana: "When you wave to someone, you should move your hand from side to side. Waving the hand up and down indicates that you consider the other person inferior to you and wish him to serve you."

All previous chiefs of protocol had been male, and they had wives to help them. Shirley was alone most of the time because her husband had his own business to run. So she didn't have such assistance. Chief of protocol was not her favorite job. One reason was that the work involved attending many parties, and she didn't particularly like parties. Some diplomats and their wives did not quite know what to make of a woman chief of protocol. The wife of one head of state insisted that Shirley do her hair!

One protocol staff member told Anne Edwards, the author of *Shirley Temple: American Princess,* "You know, she had a way of chuckling—with her chin tucked in and her eyes wide—that suddenly dissolved the distance of years. There she was, little Shirley, telling gruff old Lionel Barrymore, one of the tough guys in her early movies, in simple terms how to be happy. It was very disconcerting. She is surprisingly wise and never wishy-washy."

Shirley was also in charge of the foreign diplomats' participation in the inauguration ceremonies and inaugural ball for President Jimmy Carter. She would have gladly campaigned for Republican Gerald Ford if her job had allowed her to. Instead, she had to plan the celebrations for the new Democratic president.

In the middle of the intricate preparations, Shirley's mother, Gertrude Temple, died in California. Even so, the inauguration went as it should have. Afterward, the new president accepted Shirley Temple Black's resignation and she returned to California to relax for the first time in several years.

## Ever the Diplomat

Shirley Temple Black had hoped that she would be appointed as ambassador when Ronald Reagan was elected president. Perhaps he could never get past his memory of her as a child appearing in a movie with him. But he failed to name her to anything but various commissions.

That did not keep her out of the diplomatic

arena. Shirley Temple Black was a founding member and officer of the Board of Directors of the American Academy of Diplomacy in Washington, D.C. Only one hundred men and women are members of the academy at any one time, and they must be people who have held positions of major responsibility in regard to U.S. foreign policy. She was (and still is) an active member of the Institute of International Studies, which meets at Stanford University near her home in Woodside, California.

Since she left her post as chief of protocol, Shirley wrote her autobiography, *Child Star.* It took at least eight years to write, but it is filled with fascinating and humorous details of her life. Many little stories had never been revealed before. Only Shirley Temple herself could have written it. James Brady, reviewing the book for *Parade Magazine,* said, "It's smashing. . . . Not only funny, touching, and gossipy, it's also her own."

In 1988, Shirley Temple Black received an honor even greater than the adult-sized Oscar she was given in 1985. Secretary of State George Schultz appointed her Honorary Foreign Service Officer. This was a gesture of great esteem, making her, in effect, an equal to a fully experienced

*Black put a lot of work into her autobiography,* Child Star, *which was published in 1988.*

diplomat who had spent an entire career with the Foreign Service.

She assumed that her days as an ambassador were over, until President George Bush nominated her to be ambassador to Czechoslovakia. Her nomination was brought before the Senate Foreign Relations Committee, which has the right of approval of such appointments. Senator Daniel Patrick Moynihan of New York, who had scoffed at some of President Bush's appointments of inexperienced people, said, "It is such a great pleasure to have before the committee an experienced diplomat and a person with a very special capacity for the task she is about to undertake."

## The Velvet Revolution

Twenty-one years after Shirley Temple Black escaped from Prague during the Soviet takeover, she was back in Czechoslovakia as U.S. ambassador. The country was still controlled by the Soviet Union. This would be a very different job for her than the one in Ghana had been.

Even as she was reporting for duty in August 1989, at the seventeenth-century palace that is the U.S. embassy in Prague, change was brewing in the

Soviet Union. It's one of the primary jobs of an ambassador to keep the United States government informed of what is happening in the nation to which she is appointed. Shirley Temple Black's main job for several months was to pick up whispers of growing protests against the Communist government and relay them to Washington.

There were many whispers, because people knew change was coming. Playwright Vaclav Havel, who had been imprisoned by the Communists, had to be smuggled into the American Embassy to see Ambassador Black. The two of them discussed the probable upcoming events and America's likely reaction. Within days of Havel's visit, a massive demonstration by Czech students was joined by hundreds of thousands of workers. The continuing pressure led to the overthrow of the Czech Communist regime in November 1989.

Some of the Soviet-controlled nations, after throwing out the Communist governments, promptly fought civil wars. Rumania had a brief but very bloody war. The regions of Yugoslavia that separated into Bosnia and Federal Republic of Yugoslavia continue to fight.

Czechoslovakia, too, had been an artificial

*Ambassador Shirley Temple Black with Vaclav Havel at a celebration in Czechoslovakia*

pasting together of the Czech people and the Slovak people after World War I. When Vaclav Havel was elected president of the newly free nation, there was no war. Havel himself called it the "Velvet Revolution." The following year, Ambassador Black was influential in his winning the Nobel Peace Prize.

Havel oversaw the peaceful division of Czechoslovakia into the Czech Republic and Slovakia. On January 1, 1993, just after Shirley Temple Black returned to the United States, they each became an independent, democratic nation. Twenty-one years of Soviet domination had ended. Shirley Temple Black had been in Prague to see both the beginning and the end.

## Honoring the Honorable

The book *Child Star* took Shirley's autobiography only up to the early years of her marriage to Charles Black. Of course, her whole career in foreign relations was still ahead of her. Since leaving Czechoslovakia in 1992, the Honorable Shirley Temple Black has been working on another book about her second career.

The rewards from her first career are still coming in. When the Academy Awards were given in 1998, part of the television broadcast was an appearance by as many past winners as possible. Shirley Temple attended, feeling pleasantly inconspicuous among such famous actors as Sean Connery and Robin Williams. When her name was announced, she got more applause than anyone else. And when the telecast was over, it was to Shirley that all the other famous actors and actresses ran, hoping for a chance to meet her.

Because of video, more people today see Shirley Temple's movies than saw them when they first came out. Most people easily separate in their minds "Little Shirley," the famous, immortal child star and Shirley Temple Black, the bright, vivacious, impressive diplomat.

In 1998, Shirley Temple was one of the people honored by the John F. Kennedy Center for the Performing Arts in Washington, D.C., for her lifetime of achievement to the United States and the world of the arts.

In 1999, she was voted eighteenth among the top actresses before 1950 by the American Film Institute. Shirley Temple is almost as famous now as she was in the 1930s. Most of the forty-four

*A happy occasion. Black was accompanied by her son and husband to the 1998 gala at the John F. Kennedy Center for the Performing Arts.*

*With the other Kennedy Center honorees: Bill Cosby, John Kander, Fred Ebb, and Willie Nelson (standing, left to right) and Andre Previn (seated)*

feature films she made are still available. Two new generations of moviegoers and video watchers have come to love the child who could sing and dance, and sparkle.

Shirley Temple Black doesn't ignore her childhood movies. She knows that her childhood stardom gave her the opportunity to become the Honorable Shirley Temple Black and represent the United States around the world.

# TIMELINE

**1928**    Shirley Temple born in Santa Monica, California, on April 23

**1932**    Makes her first movie short in January

**1934**    Signs first contract with Fox Films in February; is presented with special miniature Academy Award

**1940**    Enters Westlake School for Girls as her contract with 20th Century-Fox ended

**1943**    Signs with Selznick International

**1945**    Graduates from Westlake School; marries John Agar

**1948**    Daughter Linda Susan born

**1950**    Contract with Twentieth Century-Fox ends; divorces John Agar; marries Charles Black

**1952**    Son Charles Alden Black Jr. born

**1954**    Daugher Lori Alden Black born

**1958**    TV series *Shirley Temple's Storybook* begins

| 1960 | Actively supports Richard Nixon's losing presidential campaign |
|------|------|
| 1961 | New TV series, *Shirley Temple Theater*, starts; cofounds National Federation of Multiple Sclerosis Societies |
| 1965 | Travels to the Soviet Union on behalf of the Multiple Sclerosis Federation |
| 1967 | Runs for Congress from California; comes in second |
| 1968 | Campaigns for Richard Nixon for president among Americans living abroad |
| 1969 | Is named by Governor Ronald Reagan to the California Advisory Hospital Council; is named by President Richard Nixon to be a delegate to the 24th General Assembly of the United Nations |
| 1972 | Is named by the Secretary of State to be a U.S. delegate to the UN Conference on Human Environment in Stockholm; is named special assistant to the chairman, American Council on Environmental Quality |
| 1973 | Is named a member of the U.S. Commission for UNESCO |
| 1974 | Is elected a member of the board of directors of Walt Disney Productions; is appointed by President Gerald R. Ford as ambassador to the African nation of Ghana |
| 1976 | Leaves post in Ghana to become the first female |

U.S. chief of protocol by appointment of President Ford

| | |
|---|---|
| **1981** | Is appointed a member of the U.S. Delegation on African Refugee Problems |
| **1985** | Is presented with a real Oscar at the Academy of Motion Picture Arts and Sciences "Tribute to Shirley Temple" |
| **1989** | Is appointed by President George Bush ambassador to the Czechoslovak Socialist Republic |
| **1992** | Leaves her position in Czechoslovakia |
| **1999** | Is chosen the eighteenth most popular actress from before 1950 by the American Film Institute |

# HOW TO
# BECOME AN
# ACTOR

## The Job

Actors play parts or roles in dramatic productions on the stage, in motion pictures, or on television or radio. They impersonate, or portray, characters by speech, gesture, song, and dance. The imitation of a character for presentation to an audience often seems like a glamorous and easy job. In reality, it is demanding, tiring work requiring special talents.

The actor must first find a part available in some upcoming production. This may be in a comedy, drama, musical, or opera. Then, the actor must audition before the director and other people who have control of the production. This requirement is often waived for established artists. In film and television, actors must also complete screen tests, which are scenes recorded on film, at times performed with other actors, which are later viewed by the director and producer of the film.

If selected for the part, the actor must spend hundreds of hours in rehearsal and must memorize many lines and cues. This is especially true in live theater; in film and television, actors may spend less time in rehearsal and sometimes improvise their lines before the camera, often performing several attempts, or "takes," before the director is satisfied. Actors on television often take advantage of teleprompters, which scroll their lines on a screen in front of them while performing. Radio actors generally read from a script, and therefore rehearsal times are usually shorter.

Actors in the theater may perform the same part many times a week for weeks, months, and sometimes years. This allows them to develop the role, but it can also become tedious. Actors in films may spend several weeks involved in a production, which often takes place on location—that is, in different parts of the world. Television actors involved in a series, such as a soap opera or a situation comedy, also may play the same role for years. For these actors, however, their lines change from week to week and even from day to day, and much time is spent rehearsing their new lines.

While studying and perfecting their craft, many actors work as extras, the nonspeaking characters who appear in the background on screen or stage. Many actors also continue their training. A great deal of an actor's time is spent attending auditions.

## Requirements
***High School*** There are no minimum educational requirements to become an actor. However, at least a high school diploma is recommended.

***Postsecondary*** As acting becomes more and more involved with the various facets of our society, a college degree will become more important to those who hope to have an acting career. It is assumed that the actor who has completed a liberal arts program is more capable of understanding the wide variety of roles that are available. Therefore, it is strongly recommended that aspiring actors complete at least a bachelor's degree program in theater or the dramatic arts. In addition, graduate degrees in the fine arts or in drama are nearly always required should the individual decide to teach dramatic arts. College can also serve to provide acting experience for the hopeful actor. Actors and directors recommend that those interested in acting gain as much experience as possible through acting in plays in high school and college or in those offered by community groups. Training beyond college is recommended, especially for actors interested in entering the theater. Joining acting workshops, such as the Actors Studio, can often be highly competitive.

## Exploring

The best way to explore this career is to participate in school or local theater productions. Even working on the props or lighting crew will provide insight into the field. Also, attend as many dramatic productions as possible and try to talk with people who either are currently in the theater or have been at one time. They can offer advice to individuals interested in a career in the theater.

## Employers

Motion pictures, television, and the stage are the largest fields of employment for actors, with television commercials representing as much as 60 percent of all acting jobs. Most of the opportunities for employment in these fields are either in Los Angeles or in New York. On stage, even the road shows often begin in New York, with the selection of actors conducted there along with rehearsals. However, nearly every city and most communities present local and regional theater productions.

The lowest numbers of actors are employed for stage work. In addition to Broadway shows and regional theater, there are employment opportunities for stage actors in summer stock, at resorts, and on cruise ships.

## Starting Out

Probably the best way to enter acting is to start with high school, local, or college productions and to gain as much experience as possible on that level. Very rarely is an inexperienced actor given an opportunity to perform on stage or in film in New York or Hollywood. The field is extremely difficult to enter; the more experience and ability beginners have, however, the greater the possibilities for entrance.

Those venturing to New York or Hollywood are encouraged first to have enough money to support themselves during the long waiting and searching period normally required before a job is found. Most will list themselves with a casting agency that will help them find a part as an extra or a bit player, either in theater or film. These agencies keep names on file along with photographs and a description of the individual's features and experience, and if a part comes along that may be suitable, they contact that person.

## Advancement

New actors will normally start in bit parts and will have only a few, if any, lines to speak. The normal procession of advancement would then lead to larger supporting roles and then, in the case of theater, possibly to a role as understudy for one of the main actors. The understudy usually has an opportunity to fill in should the main actor be unable to give a performance. Many film and television actors get their start in commercials or by appearing in government and commercially sponsored public service announcements, films, and programs. Other actors join the afternoon soap operas and continue on to evening programs. Many actors have also gotten their start in on-camera roles such as presenting the weather segment of a local news program. Once an actor has gained experience, he or she may go on to play stronger supporting roles or even leading roles in stage, television, or film productions. From there, an actor may go on to stardom. Only a very small number of actors ever reach that pinnacle, however.

## Earnings

The wage scale for actors is largely controlled through bargaining agreements reached by various unions in negotiations with producers. These agreements normally control the minimum salaries, hours of work permitted per week, and other conditions of employment. In addition, each artist enters into a separate contract that may provide for higher salaries.

The 1997 minimum weekly salary for actors in Broadway productions was $1,040, according to the Actors' Equity Association. Minimum salaries for those performing in "Off Broadway" productions ranged from $400 to $625 a week, depending on the size of the theater. Smaller capacity theater productions paid about $375 to $600 weekly. Touring shows paid an additional $100 a day. A steady income is not the norm for most stage actors. Less than 50 percent of those belonging to the Actors' Equity Association found stage work in 1996; average earnings were $13,700.

According to the Screen Actors Guild, actors appearing in motion pictures or television shows were paid a daily minimum of $559, or $1,942 a week, in 1997. Extras earned a minimum of $99 a day. Motion picture actors may also receive additional payments known as residuals as part of their guaranteed salary. Many motion picture actors receive residuals whenever films, TV shows, and TV commercials in which they appear are rerun, sold for TV exhibition, or put on videocassette. Residuals often exceed the actors' original salary and account for about one-third of all actors' income.

The annual earnings of persons in television and movies are affected by frequent periods of unemployment. Most guild members earn less than $5,000 a year from acting jobs. Unions offer health, welfare, and pension fund for members working over a set number of weeks a year. Some actors are eligible for paid vacation and sick time, depending on the work contract.

## Work Environment
Actors work under varying conditions. Those employed in motion pictures may work in air-conditioned studios one week and be on location in a hot desert the next.

Those in stage productions perform under all types of

conditions. The number of hours employed per day or week vary, as do the number of weeks employed per year. Stage actors normally perform eight shows per week with any additional performances paid for as overtime. The basic workweek after the show opens is about 36 hours unless major changes in the play are needed. The number of hours worked per week is considerably more before the opening, because of rehearsals. Evening work is a natural part of a stage actor's life. Rehearsals often are held at night and over holidays and weekends. If the play goes on the road, much traveling will be involved.

A number of actors cannot receive unemployment compensation when they are waiting for their next part, primarily because they have not worked enough to meet the minimum eligibility requirements for compensation. Sick leaves and paid vacations are not usually available to the actor. However, union actors who earn the minimum qualifications now receive full medical and health insurance under all the actors' unions. Those who earn health plan benefits for 10 years become eligible for a pension upon retirement.The acting field is very uncertain. Aspirants never know whether they will be able to get into the profession, and, once in, there are uncertainties as to whether the show will be well received and, if not, whether the actors' talent can survive a bad show.

## Outlook

Jobs in acting are expected to grow faster than the average through the year 2008. There are a number of reasons for this. The growth of satellite and cable television in the past decade has created a demand for more actors, especially as the cable networks produce more and more of their own programs and films. The rise of home video has also created new acting jobs, as more and more films are made strictly for the home video market. Many resorts built in the 1980s and 1990s present their own theatrical productions, providing more job opportunities for actors. Jobs in theater, however, face pressure as the cost of mounting a production rises and as many nonprofit and smaller theaters lose their funding.

Despite the growth in opportunities, there are many more actors than there are roles, and this is likely to remain true for years to come. This is true in all areas of the arts, including radio, television, motion pictures, and theater, and even those who are employed are normally employed during only a small portion of the year. Many actors must supplement their income by working as secretaries, waiters, or taxi drivers, for example. Almost all performers are members of more than one union in order to take advantage of various opportunities as they become available.

Of the 105,000 or so actors in the United States today, only about 16,000 are employed at any one time. Of these, few are able to support themselves on their earnings from acting, and fewer still will ever achieve stardom. Most actors work for many years before becoming known, and most of these do not rise above supporting roles. The vast majority of actors, meanwhile, are still looking for the right break. There are many more applicants in all areas than there are positions. As with most careers in the arts, people enter this career out of a love of acting.

# TO LEARN MORE ABOUT ACTORS

## Books

Caruso, Sandra, and Susan Kosoff. *The Young Actor's Book of Improvisation: Dramatic Situations from Shakespeare to Spielberg.* Portsmouth, N.H.: Heinemann, 1998.

Horner, Matina S. *Elizabeth Taylor.* New York: Chelsea House, 1997.

Krohn, Katherine E. *Lucille Ball: Pioneer of Comedy.* Minneapolis: Lerner, 1992.

McAvoy, Jim. *Tom Hanks.* Broomall, Penn.: Chelsea House, 1998.

Quinlan, Kathryn A. *Actor.* Mankato, Minn.: Capstone Press, 1998.

Simmons, Alex. *Denzel Washington.* Austin, Tex.: Raintree/Steck-Vaughn, 1998.

# Websites

## Acting Workshop On-Line

*http://www.execpc.com/~blankda/acting2.html*
This site has information for beginners on acting and the acting business.

## ActorSource Homepage

http://www.actorsource.com/
For information about how to get started in acting and how to choose a monologue

# Where to Write

## Actors' Equity Association

165 West 46th Street
New York, NY 10036
For more information about the union for actors in theater and "live" industrial productions, stage managers, directors, and choreographers

## American Federation of Television and Radio Artists— Screen Actors Guild

260 Madison Avenue
New York, NY 10016
For more information about the union that represents television and radio performers

## Screen Actors Guild

5757 Wilshire Boulevard
Los Angeles, CA 90036-3600
For more information about the union that represents film and television performers

# HOW TO BECOME A FOREIGN SERVICE OFFICER

## The Job

Foreign Service Officers (FSOs) represent the government and the people of the United States by conducting relations with foreign countries and international organizations. They promote and protect the U.S. political, economic, and commercial interests overseas. They observe and analyze conditions and developments in foreign countries and report to the State Department and other agencies. They guard the welfare of Americans abroad and help foreign nationals traveling to the United States. There are about 4,000 (FSOs) in more than 250 U.S. embassies and consulates and in Washington, D.C.

The work of Foreign Service Officers is divided into four broad areas: administration, consular affairs, economic and commercial affairs, and political affairs.

Administrative officers who work in embassies and consulates manage and administer the day-to-day operations of their posts. Some handle financial matters such as planning budgets and controlling expenditures. Others work in general services: they purchase and look after government property and supplies, negotiate leases and contracts for office space and housing, and make arrangements for travel and shipping.

Consular officers help U.S. citizens abroad as well as foreigners wishing to enter the United States as visitors or residents. They provide medical, legal, personal, and travel assistance to U.S. citizens in accidents or emergencies, such as helping those without money to return home, finding lost relatives, visiting and advising those in foreign jails, and distributing social security checks to eligible people.

Economic officers study the structure of a country's economy and the way it functions to determine how the United States might be affected by trends, trade patterns, and methods of setting prices. Their analysis of the economic data.

Political officers overseas convey the positions of the United States to government officials of the countries where they are based, keep the United States informed about any political developments, and may negotiate agreements between the two governments. Political officers are alert to local developments and reactions to U.S. policy.

Political officers in Washington study the information submitted by their counterparts abroad. They keep State Department and White House officials informed of developments overseas and the possible effects on the United

States. They suggest revisions in U.S. policy and see that officers abroad carry out approved changes.

The U.S. Information Service assigns information officers and cultural officers to serve at diplomatic missions in foreign countries. Information officers prepare and disseminate information designed to help other countries understand the United States and its policies.

Cultural officers engage in activities that promote an understanding and appreciation of American culture and traditions. These activities may involve educational and cultural exchanges between the countries, exhibits, lectures, performing arts events, libraries, book translations, English teaching programs, and youth groups.

## Requirements

**High School**   Working for the Foreign Service will call upon a great deal of general knowledge about the world and its history. Take courses such as social studies, U.S. government, and English literature. English composition will help you develop writing and communication skills. Any foreign language course will give you a good foundation in language study—and can help in getting a job with the Foreign Service and earn you a higher starting salary.

**Postsecondary**   Though the Foreign Service is open to any U.S. citizen who is between the ages of twenty-one and fifty-nine who passes the written, oral, and physical examinations, you'll need at least a bachelor's degree to be competitive. Most Foreign Service Officers have graduate degrees. Regardless of the level of education, candidates are expected to have a broad knowledge of foreign and domestic affairs and be well informed on U.S.

history, government, economics, culture, literature, and business administration. The fields of study most often chosen by those with a higher education include history, international relations, political science, economics, law, English literature, and foreign languages. The Foreign Service has internship opportunities available to college students in their junior and senior years and to graduate students. About half of these unpaid internships are based in Washington, D.C., while the other half are at U.S. embassies and consulates overseas. As an intern, you may write reports, assist with trade negotiations, or work with budget projects. You may be involved in visa or passport work. The Foreign Service also offers a Foreign Affairs Fellowship Program, which provides funding to undergraduate and graduate students preparing to enter the Foreign Service.

## Exploring

As a member of a foreign language club at your school, you may have the opportunity to visit other countries. If such programs don't exist, check with your guidance counselor about discounted foreign travel packages available to student groups. Also ask them about student exchange programs.

The American Foreign Service Association (AFSA), a professional association serving Foreign Service Officers, publishes the *Foreign Service Journal (FSJ)*. The *FSJ* features articles by Foreign Service Officers and academics which can give you insight into the Foreign Service.

## Employers

The Foreign Service isn't a single organization, so you'll

actually be applying to join one of two different agencies: either the Department of State or the U.S. Information Agency (USIA). The Department of State is responsible for the development and implementation of foreign policy, while the USIA explains these policies and actions to the world by engaging in public diplomacy. When hired, you'll be offered an appointment to one of these agencies. There's very little moving about between agencies. You'll either work in Washington, D.C., or you'll be stationed in one of the approximately 170 foreign countries that have U.S. embassies or consulates.

## Starting Out

Many people apply to the Foreign Service directly after finishing graduate school, while others work in other government agencies or professions. Some serve with the Peace Corps or the military, gaining experience with foreign affairs before applying, or they work as teachers in American-sponsored schools overseas. Some work as Congressional aides or interns.

Before being offered a job with the Foreign Service, you have to pass a series of tests. The U.S. State Department offers a study guide to help applicants prepare for the exam. The number of positions available varies from year to year; typically, thousands of people apply for fewer than 100 positions. The Foreign Service has been known to cancel its annual exam because of too few job openings.

Those who pass the written exam move on to the oral interview and must pass a security clearance and a medical exam. But passing these tests doesn't necessarily mean employment—your name is placed on a rank-order list of eligible candidates based on your test scores.

## Advancement

New recruits are given a temporary appointment as career candidates, or junior officers. This probationary period lasts no longer than five years and consists of orientation and work overseas. During this time all junior officers must learn a foreign language. The candidate's performance will be reviewed after thirty-six months of service, at which time a decision on tenure (once tenured, an officer can't be separated from the service without written cause) and appointment as a career Foreign Service Officer will be made. If tenure is not granted, the candidate will be reviewed again approximately one year later. Those who fail to show potential as career officers are dropped from the program.

## Earnings

Foreign Service Officers are paid on a sliding scale. The exact figures depend on their qualifications and experience. In 1998, the approximate starting salary for new appointees without a bachelor's degree was $27,951 a year. Bachelor's and advanced degrees, and knowledge of a foreign language, can earn you a greater salary. Junior officers make up to $56,665 a year. Career officers make between $47,619 and $94,927, while senior Foreign Service Officers make $99,200 to $118,400.

Benefits are usually generous, although they vary from post to post. Officers are housed free of charge or given a housing allowance. They receive a cost-of-living allowance, higher pay if they work in an area that imposes undue hardship on them and their families, medical and retirement benefits, and an education allowance for their children.

## Work Environment

Foreign Service Officers may be assigned to work in Washington, D.C., or in any embassy or consulate in the world. They generally spend about 60 percent of their time abroad and are transferred every two to four years.

Most offices overseas are clean, pleasant, and well equipped. But Foreign Service Officers sometimes have to travel into areas that may present health hazards. Customs may differ considerably, medical care may be substandard or nonexistent, and the climate may be extreme. In some countries there is the danger of earthquakes, typhoons, or floods; in others, the danger of political upheaval.

## Outlook

The heavy competition and extensive testing mentioned above aren't the only obstacles to getting work with the Foreign Service. In the last decade, the U.S. international affairs budget has been drastically cut. Foreign aid funding has dropped from $20 billion in 1985 to $12.4 billion in 1995. Seventeen U.S. embassies and consulates were closed between 1991 and 1995. Those people interested in protecting diplomacy and the strength of the Foreign Service need to follow relevant legislation closely, as well as promote the importance of international affairs.

# TO LEARN MORE ABOUT FOREIGN SERVICE OFFICERS

## Books

Armbruster, Ann. *The United Nations.* Danbury, Conn.: Franklin Watts, 1997.

Burger, Leslie. *United Nations High Commissioner for Refugees: Making a Difference in Our World.* Minneapolis: Lerner, 1996.

Hasday, Judy L. *Madeleine Albright.* Broomall, Penn.: Chelsea House, 1998.

Schraff, Anne E. *Ralph J. Bunch: Winner of the Nobel Peace Prize.* Springfield, N.J.: Enslow, 1999.

Stein, R. Conrad. *The United Nations.* Chicago: Childrens Press, 1994.

## Websites
### American Foreign Service Association
*http://www.afsa.org*
To browse an informative website about the work of Foreign Service Officers

### U.S. Department of State
*http://www.state.gov*
For a wealth of career information, along with information about internships, the history of the Foreign Service, and current officers and embassies

## Where to Write
### American Foreign Service Association
2101 E Street, N.W.
Washington, DC 20037
A professional organization serving current and retired Foreign Service Officers

### Foreign Service
### U.S. Department of State
P.O. Box 9317
Rosslyn Station
Arlington, VA 22219
For brochures about a career in Foreign Service

# TO LEARN MORE ABOUT SHIRLEY TEMPLE BLACK

## Books

Fiori, Carlo. *The Story of Shirley Temple Black: Hollywood's Youngest Star.* Milwaukee: Gareth Stevens, 1997.

Haskins, James. *Shirley Temple Black: Actress to Ambassador.* New York: Puffin, 1988.

## Websites

**Kennedy Center Honors Shirley Temple Black**
*http://www.kennedy-center.org/honors/years/temple_black.html*
For a thorough overview of Shirley Temple Black's career

**NASA's Women of the World**
*http://www.quest.arc.nasa.gov/women/bios/black.html*
For archived online interviews and an overview of Shirley Temple Black's career

**Shirley Temple Fans**
*http://shirleytemplefans.com/f1.htm*
For links and extensive information about Shirley Temple
Black, her career, and other fan sites

## Interesting Places to Visit
**Mann's Chinese Theatre**
6925 Hollywood Boulevard
Hollywood, CA
323/464-6266
To visit this famous theater and see the handprints and
footprints of well-known film stars, including Shirley Temple, preserved in cement

**Smithsonian**
**National Museum of American History**
14th Street and Constitution Avenue, N.W.
Washington, DC 20560
202/357-2700
To see exhibits on American social and cultural history as
well as sheet music from some of Shirley Temple's films

# INDEX

Page numbers in *italics* indicate illustrations.

**125**

# ABOUT THE AUTHOR

Jean Blashfield has written about ninety books, most of them for young people. She likes best to write about interesting places, but she loves history and science too. In fact, one of her big advantages as a writer is that she becomes fascinated by just about every subject she investigates. She has created an encyclopedia of aviation and space, written popular books on murderers and house plants, and had a lot of fun creating an early book on the things women have done, called *Hellraisers, Heroines, and Holy Women.*

In Wisconsin, she delighted in finding TSR, Inc., the publishers of the *Dungeons & Dragons* games. At that company, she founded a new department to publish fantasy gamebooks and novels and helped the company expand into a worldwide enterprise.

Ms. Blashfield lives in Delavan, Wisconsin.